MY KAYAKING LOG BOOK

NAME:

ADDRESS:

EMAIL:

PHONE:

BIRTHDAY:

MY GOALS ✓

1- ☐

2- ☐

3- ☐

4- ☐

5- ☐

MY STRATEGIES ☰

MY GOALS ✓

6- ☐

7- ☐

8- ☐

9- ☐

10- ☐

MY STRATEGIES

📅 DATE:	TIME:

📍 STARTING POINT:

✓ DESTINATION:

🕐 DISTANCE:

⏱ DURATION:

👥 TEAM / PADDLE PARTNER

☐	☐
☐	☐
☐	☐

GEAR / EQUIPMENT

WEATHER CONDITIONS

TEMPERATURE _____ ☀ ⛅ ☁ 🌧 ❄

WIND _____ ☐ ☐ ☐ ☐ ☐

WATER VISIBILITY

CLEAR	1	2	3	4	5	MISTY
	☐	☐	☐	☐	☐	

BODY OF WATER

☐ LAKE	☐ OCEAN	☐ CANAL
☐ SEA	☐ RIVER	☐ OTHER

TRIP GOALS

OCEAN/BUOY/SURF/MARINE:

📍 STOPS	🕐 TIME OF ARRIVAL	📄 OBSERVATIONS

ADDITIONAL NOTES

_____

_____

_____

_____

_____

DATE: **TIME:**

STARTING POINT:

DESTINATION:

DISTANCE:

DURATION:

TEAM / PADDLE PARTNER

☐	☐
☐	☐
☐	☐

GEAR / EQUIPMENT

WEATHER CONDITIONS

TEMPERATURE _____ ☀ ⛅ ☁ 🌧 ❄

WIND _____ ☐ ☐ ☐ ☐ ☐

WATER VISIBILITY

1	2	3	4	5

CLEAR   MISTY

☐   ☐   ☐   ☐   ☐

BODY OF WATER

◻ LAKE	◻ OCEAN	◻ CANAL
◻ SEA	◻ RIVER	◻ OTHER

TRIP GOALS

OCEAN/BUOY/SURF/MARINE:

STOPS	TIME OF ARRIVAL	OBSERVATIONS

ADDITIONAL NOTES

_____

_____

_____

_____

_____

	DATE:	TIME:

STARTING POINT:

DESTINATION:

DISTANCE:

DURATION:

TEAM / PADDLE PARTNER

☐	☐
☐	☐
☐	☐

GEAR / EQUIPMENT

WEATHER CONDITIONS

TEMPERATURE _____

WIND _____ ☐ ☐ ☐ ☐ ☐

WATER VISIBILITY

CLEAR 1 2 3 4 5 MISTY

☐ ☐ ☐ ☐ ☐

BODY OF WATER

	LAKE		OCEAN		CANAL
	SEA		RIVER		OTHER

TRIP GOALS

OCEAN/BUOY/SURF/MARINE:

⊘ STOPS	⊙ TIME OF ARRIVAL	🗎 OBSERVATIONS

ADDITIONAL NOTES

📅 DATE:	TIME:

📍 STARTING POINT:

📍 DESTINATION:

🕐 DISTANCE:

⏱ DURATION:

WEATHER CONDITIONS

🌡 TEMPERATURE _____ ☀ ⛅ ☁ 🌧 ❄

💨 WIND _____ ☐ ☐ ☐ ☐ ☐

WATER VISIBILITY

	1	2	3	4	5	
CLEAR						MISTY
	☐	☐	☐	☐	☐	

👥 TEAM / PADDLE PARTNER

☐	☐
☐	☐
☐	☐

BODY OF WATER

☐ LAKE	☐ OCEAN	☐ CANAL
☐ SEA	☐ RIVER	☐ OTHER

GEAR / EQUIPMENT

TRIP GOALS

OCEAN/BUOY/SURF/MARINE:

📍 STOPS	🕐 TIME OF ARRIVAL	📄 OBSERVATIONS

ADDITIONAL NOTES

	DATE:	TIME:

STARTING POINT:

DESTINATION:

DISTANCE:

DURATION:

TEAM / PADDLE PARTNER

☐	☐
☐	☐
☐	☐

GEAR / EQUIPMENT

WEATHER CONDITIONS

TEMPERATURE _____ ☀ ⛅ ☁ 🌧 ❄

WIND _____ ☐ ☐ ☐ ☐ ☐

WATER VISIBILITY

	1	2	3	4	5	
CLEAR						MISTY
	☐	☐	☐	☐	☐	

BODY OF WATER

	LAKE		OCEAN		CANAL
	SEA		RIVER		OTHER

TRIP GOALS

OCEAN/BUOY/SURF/MARINE:

📍 STOPS	🕐 TIME OF ARRIVAL	📄 OBSERVATIONS

ADDITIONAL NOTES

	DATE:	TIME:

STARTING POINT:

DESTINATION:

DISTANCE:

DURATION:

TEAM / PADDLE PARTNER

☐	☐
☐	☐
☐	☐

GEAR / EQUIPMENT

WEATHER CONDITIONS

TEMPERATURE _____ ☀ ⛅ ☁ 🌧 ❄

WIND _____ ☐ ☐ ☐ ☐ ☐

WATER VISIBILITY

	1	2	3	4	5	
CLEAR						MISTY
	☐	☐	☐	☐	☐	

BODY OF WATER

☐ LAKE	☐ OCEAN	☐ CANAL
☐ SEA	☐ RIVER	☐ OTHER

TRIP GOALS

OCEAN/BUOY/SURF/MARINE:

STOPS	TIME OF ARRIVAL	OBSERVATIONS

ADDITIONAL NOTES

_____

_____

_____

_____

_____

	DATE:	TIME:

STARTING POINT:

DESTINATION:

DISTANCE:

DURATION:

TEAM / PADDLE PARTNER

☐	☐
☐	☐
☐	☐

GEAR / EQUIPMENT

WEATHER CONDITIONS

TEMPERATURE _____

WIND _____ ☐ ☐ ☐ ☐ ☐

WATER VISIBILITY

1	2	3	4	5

CLEAR ———————————————— MISTY

☐ ☐ ☐ ☐ ☐

BODY OF WATER

	LAKE		OCEAN		CANAL
	SEA		RIVER		OTHER

TRIP GOALS

OCEAN/BUOY/SURF/MARINE:

⌖ STOPS	⏱ TIME OF ARRIVAL	🗎 OBSERVATIONS

ADDITIONAL NOTES

	DATE:	TIME:

	STARTING POINT:

	DESTINATION:

	DISTANCE:

	DURATION:

WEATHER CONDITIONS

TEMPERATURE _____

WIND _____

WATER VISIBILITY

CLEAR	1	2	3	4	5	MISTY
	☐	☐	☐	☐	☐	

TEAM / PADDLE PARTNER

☐	☐
☐	☐
☐	☐

BODY OF WATER

	LAKE		OCEAN		CANAL
	SEA		RIVER		OTHER

GEAR / EQUIPMENT

TRIP GOALS

OCEAN/BUOY/SURF/MARINE:

STOPS	TIME OF ARRIVAL	OBSERVATIONS

ADDITIONAL NOTES

DATE:	TIME:

STARTING POINT:

DESTINATION:

DISTANCE:

DURATION:

TEAM / PADDLE PARTNER

☐	☐
☐	☐
☐	☐

GEAR / EQUIPMENT

WEATHER CONDITIONS

TEMPERATURE ___	☀	⛅	☁	🌧	❄
WIND ___	☐	☐	☐	☐	☐

WATER VISIBILITY

	1	2	3	4	5	
CLEAR						MISTY
	☐	☐	☐	☐	☐	

BODY OF WATER

	LAKE		OCEAN		CANAL
	SEA		RIVER		OTHER

TRIP GOALS

OCEAN/BUOY/SURF/MARINE:

◉ STOPS	⏱ TIME OF ARRIVAL	📄 OBSERVATIONS

ADDITIONAL NOTES

📅 DATE:	TIME:

📍 **STARTING POINT:**

📍 **DESTINATION:**

🕐 **DISTANCE:**

⏱ **DURATION:**

👥 TEAM / PADDLE PARTNER

☐	☐
☐	☐
☐	☐

GEAR / EQUIPMENT

WEATHER CONDITIONS

🌡 TEMPERATURE _____ ☀ ⛅ ☁ 🌧 ❄

🗔 WIND _____ ☐ ☐ ☐ ☐ ☐

WATER VISIBILITY

1	2	3	4	5
CLEAR ▭▭▭▭▭ MISTY

☐ ☐ ☐ ☐ ☐

BODY OF WATER

▦ LAKE	▦ OCEAN	▦ CANAL
▦ SEA	▦ RIVER	▦ OTHER

TRIP GOALS

OCEAN/BUOY/SURF/MARINE:

📍 STOPS	🕐 TIME OF ARRIVAL	📄 OBSERVATIONS

ADDITIONAL NOTES

_____

_____

_____

_____

_____

DATE: TIME:	**WEATHER CONDITIONS**
STARTING POINT:	TEMPERATURE _____ ☼ ⛅ ☁ 🌧 ❄
DESTINATION:	WIND _____ ☐ ☐ ☐ ☐ ☐
DISTANCE:	**WATER VISIBILITY**
DURATION:	CLEAR 1 2 3 4 5 MISTY ☐ ☐ ☐ ☐ ☐

TEAM / PADDLE PARTNER

☐	☐
☐	☐
☐	☐

BODY OF WATER

LAKE	OCEAN	CANAL
SEA	RIVER	OTHER

GEAR / EQUIPMENT

TRIP GOALS

OCEAN/BUOY/SURF/MARINE:

STOPS	TIME OF ARRIVAL	OBSERVATIONS

ADDITIONAL NOTES

DATE: **TIME:**

STARTING POINT:

DESTINATION:

DISTANCE:

DURATION:

TEAM / PADDLE PARTNER

☐	☐
☐	☐
☐	☐

GEAR / EQUIPMENT

WEATHER CONDITIONS

TEMPERATURE _____ ☼ ⛅ ☁ 🌧 ❄

WIND _____ ☐ ☐ ☐ ☐ ☐

WATER VISIBILITY

	1	2	3	4	5	
CLEAR						MISTY
	☐	☐	☐	☐	☐	

BODY OF WATER

	LAKE		OCEAN		CANAL
	SEA		RIVER		OTHER

TRIP GOALS

OCEAN/BUOY/SURF/MARINE:

⊘ STOPS	🕐 TIME OF ARRIVAL	🗎 OBSERVATIONS

ADDITIONAL NOTES

DATE: TIME:	**WEATHER CONDITIONS**
STARTING POINT:	TEMPERATURE _____ ☼ ⛅ ☁ 🌧 ❄
DESTINATION:	WIND _____ ☐ ☐ ☐ ☐ ☐
DISTANCE:	**WATER VISIBILITY**
DURATION:	1 2 3 4 5

TEAM / PADDLE PARTNER

☐	☐
☐	☐
☐	☐

WATER VISIBILITY

CLEAR |_____| MISTY
1 2 3 4 5
☐ ☐ ☐ ☐ ☐

BODY OF WATER

☐ LAKE	☐ OCEAN	☐ CANAL
☐ SEA	☐ RIVER	☐ OTHER

GEAR / EQUIPMENT

TRIP GOALS

OCEAN/BUOY/SURF/MARINE:

⊘ STOPS	⊙ TIME OF ARRIVAL	🗎 OBSERVATIONS

ADDITIONAL NOTES

_____

_____

_____

_____

_____

DATE:	TIME:

STARTING POINT:

DESTINATION:

DISTANCE:

DURATION:

TEAM / PADDLE PARTNER

☐	☐
☐	☐
☐	☐

GEAR / EQUIPMENT

WEATHER CONDITIONS

TEMPERATURE _____	☼	⛅	☁	🌧	❄
WIND _____	☐	☐	☐	☐	☐

WATER VISIBILITY

CLEAR	1	2	3	4	5	MISTY
	☐	☐	☐	☐	☐	

BODY OF WATER

	LAKE		OCEAN		CANAL
	SEA		RIVER		OTHER

TRIP GOALS

OCEAN/BUOY/SURF/MARINE:

⦿ STOPS	🕐 TIME OF ARRIVAL	📄 OBSERVATIONS

ADDITIONAL NOTES

_____

_____

_____

_____

_____

📅 DATE:	TIME:

📍 STARTING POINT:

📍 DESTINATION:

🕐 DISTANCE:

⏱ DURATION:

WEATHER CONDITIONS

🌡 TEMPERATURE _____ ☀ ⛅ ☁ 🌧 ❄

🌊 WIND _____ ☐ ☐ ☐ ☐ ☐

WATER VISIBILITY

	1	2	3	4	5	
CLEAR						MISTY
	☐	☐	☐	☐	☐	

TEAM / PADDLE PARTNER

☐	☐
☐	☐
☐	☐

BODY OF WATER

▢ LAKE	▢ OCEAN	▢ CANAL
▢ SEA	▢ RIVER	▢ OTHER

GEAR / EQUIPMENT

TRIP GOALS

OCEAN/BUOY/SURF/MARINE:

📍 STOPS	🕐 TIME OF ARRIVAL	📄 OBSERVATIONS

ADDITIONAL NOTES

_____
_____
_____
_____
_____

📅 DATE:	TIME:

📍 STARTING POINT:

✓ DESTINATION:

⏱ DISTANCE:

⏱ DURATION:

WEATHER CONDITIONS

🌡 TEMPERATURE _____ ☀ ⛅ ☁ 🌧 ❄

📶 WIND _____ ☐ ☐ ☐ ☐ ☐

WATER VISIBILITY

	1	2	3	4	5	
CLEAR						MISTY
	☐	☐	☐	☐	☐	

TEAM / PADDLE PARTNER

☐	☐
☐	☐
☐	☐

BODY OF WATER

LAKE	OCEAN	CANAL
SEA	RIVER	OTHER

GEAR / EQUIPMENT

TRIP GOALS

OCEAN/BUOY/SURF/MARINE:

📍 STOPS	🕐 TIME OF ARRIVAL	📄 OBSERVATIONS

ADDITIONAL NOTES

DATE: **TIME:**

STARTING POINT:

DESTINATION:

DISTANCE:

DURATION:

TEAM / PADDLE PARTNER

☐	☐
☐	☐
☐	☐

GEAR / EQUIPMENT

WEATHER CONDITIONS

TEMPERATURE _____ ☀ ⛅ ☁ 🌧 ❄

WIND _____ ☐ ☐ ☐ ☐ ☐

WATER VISIBILITY

CLEAR 1 2 3 4 5 MISTY
☐ ☐ ☐ ☐ ☐

BODY OF WATER

☐ LAKE	☐ OCEAN	☐ CANAL
☐ SEA	☐ RIVER	☐ OTHER

TRIP GOALS

OCEAN/BUOY/SURF/MARINE:

📍 STOPS	🕐 TIME OF ARRIVAL	📄 OBSERVATIONS

ADDITIONAL NOTES

DATE:	TIME:

STARTING POINT:

DESTINATION:

DISTANCE:

DURATION:

TEAM / PADDLE PARTNER

☐	☐
☐	☐
☐	☐

GEAR / EQUIPMENT

WEATHER CONDITIONS

TEMPERATURE ___	☀	⛅	☁	🌧	❄
WIND ___	☐	☐	☐	☐	☐

WATER VISIBILITY

1	2	3	4	5
CLEAR				MISTY
☐	☐	☐	☐	☐

BODY OF WATER

LAKE	OCEAN	CANAL
SEA	RIVER	OTHER

TRIP GOALS

OCEAN/BUOY/SURF/MARINE:

STOPS	TIME OF ARRIVAL	OBSERVATIONS

ADDITIONAL NOTES

_____
_____
_____
_____
_____

DATE:	TIME:

STARTING POINT:

DESTINATION:

DISTANCE:

DURATION:

WEATHER CONDITIONS

TEMPERATURE _____

WIND _____ ☐ ☐ ☐ ☐ ☐

WATER VISIBILITY

CLEAR 1 2 3 4 5 MISTY

☐ ☐ ☐ ☐ ☐

TEAM / PADDLE PARTNER

☐	☐
☐	☐
☐	☐

BODY OF WATER

LAKE	OCEAN	CANAL
SEA	RIVER	OTHER

GEAR / EQUIPMENT

TRIP GOALS

OCEAN/BUOY/SURF/MARINE:

⊘ STOPS	⊘ TIME OF ARRIVAL	📄 OBSERVATIONS

ADDITIONAL NOTES

📅 DATE:	TIME:

📍 STARTING POINT:

✅ DESTINATION:

🕐 DISTANCE:

⏱ DURATION:

WEATHER CONDITIONS

🌡 TEMPERATURE _____ ☀ ⛅ ☁ 🌧 ❄

💨 WIND _____ ☐ ☐ ☐ ☐ ☐

WATER VISIBILITY

	1	2	3	4	5	
CLEAR						MISTY
	☐	☐	☐	☐	☐	

👥 TEAM / PADDLE PARTNER

☐	☐
☐	☐
☐	☐

BODY OF WATER

▦ LAKE	▦ OCEAN	▦ CANAL
▦ SEA	▦ RIVER	▦ OTHER

GEAR / EQUIPMENT

TRIP GOALS

OCEAN/BUOY/SURF/MARINE:

📍 STOPS	🕐 TIME OF ARRIVAL	📄 OBSERVATIONS

ADDITIONAL NOTES

DATE: TIME:

STARTING POINT:

DESTINATION:

DISTANCE:

DURATION:

TEAM / PADDLE PARTNER

☐	☐
☐	☐
☐	☐

GEAR / EQUIPMENT

WEATHER CONDITIONS

TEMPERATURE _____ ☀ ⛅ ☁ 🌧 ❄

WIND _____ ☐ ☐ ☐ ☐ ☐

WATER VISIBILITY

1	2	3	4	5
CLEAR   MISTY

☐   ☐   ☐   ☐   ☐

BODY OF WATER

■ LAKE	■ OCEAN	■ CANAL
■ SEA	■ RIVER	■ OTHER

TRIP GOALS

OCEAN/BUOY/SURF/MARINE:

⬇ STOPS	🕐 TIME OF ARRIVAL	📄 OBSERVATIONS

ADDITIONAL NOTES

_____

_____

_____

_____

_____

DATE: TIME:

STARTING POINT:

DESTINATION:

DISTANCE:

DURATION:

TEAM / PADDLE PARTNER

☐	☐
☐	☐
☐	☐

GEAR / EQUIPMENT

WEATHER CONDITIONS

TEMPERATURE _____ ☀ ⛅ ☁ 🌧 ❄

WIND _____ ☐ ☐ ☐ ☐ ☐

WATER VISIBILITY

1	2	3	4	5
CLEAR				MISTY
☐	☐	☐	☐	☐

BODY OF WATER

LAKE	OCEAN	CANAL
SEA	RIVER	OTHER

TRIP GOALS

OCEAN/BUOY/SURF/MARINE:

⊘ STOPS	🕐 TIME OF ARRIVAL	📄 OBSERVATIONS

ADDITIONAL NOTES

_____

_____

_____

_____

_____

	DATE:	TIME:

	STARTING POINT:

	DESTINATION:

	DISTANCE:

	DURATION:

TEAM / PADDLE PARTNER

☐	☐
☐	☐
☐	☐

GEAR / EQUIPMENT

WEATHER CONDITIONS

TEMPERATURE _____	☀	⛅	☁	🌧	❄
WIND _____	☐	☐	☐	☐	☐

WATER VISIBILITY

CLEAR |1   2   3   4   5| MISTY

☐	☐	☐	☐	☐

BODY OF WATER

	LAKE		OCEAN		CANAL
	SEA		RIVER		OTHER

TRIP GOALS

OCEAN/BUOY/SURF/MARINE:

📍 STOPS	🕐 TIME OF ARRIVAL	📄 OBSERVATIONS

ADDITIONAL NOTES

DATE:	TIME:

STARTING POINT:

DESTINATION:

DISTANCE:

DURATION:

TEAM / PADDLE PARTNER

☐	☐
☐	☐
☐	☐

GEAR / EQUIPMENT

WEATHER CONDITIONS

TEMPERATURE _____ ☼ ⛅ ☁ 🌧 ❄

WIND _____ ☐ ☐ ☐ ☐ ☐

WATER VISIBILITY

	1	2	3	4	5	
CLEAR						MISTY
	☐	☐	☐	☐	☐	

BODY OF WATER

	LAKE		OCEAN		CANAL
	SEA		RIVER		OTHER

TRIP GOALS

OCEAN/BUOY/SURF/MARINE:

⊘ STOPS	⊘ TIME OF ARRIVAL	▤ OBSERVATIONS

ADDITIONAL NOTES

_____

_____

_____

_____

_____

	DATE:	TIME:

STARTING POINT:

DESTINATION:

DISTANCE:

DURATION:

WEATHER CONDITIONS

TEMPERATURE _____

WIND _____

WATER VISIBILITY

CLEAR | 1 | 2 | 3 | 4 | 5 | MISTY

☐ ☐ ☐ ☐ ☐

TEAM / PADDLE PARTNER

☐	☐
☐	☐
☐	☐

BODY OF WATER

	LAKE		OCEAN		CANAL
	SEA		RIVER		OTHER

GEAR / EQUIPMENT

TRIP GOALS

OCEAN/BUOY/SURF/MARINE:

⊘ STOPS	🕐 TIME OF ARRIVAL	📄 OBSERVATIONS

ADDITIONAL NOTES

_____

_____

_____

_____

_____

	DATE:	TIME:

STARTING POINT:

DESTINATION:

DISTANCE:

DURATION:

TEAM / PADDLE PARTNER

☐	☐
☐	☐
☐	☐

GEAR / EQUIPMENT

WEATHER CONDITIONS

TEMPERATURE ____ ☀ ⛅ ☁ 🌧 ❄

WIND ____ ☐ ☐ ☐ ☐ ☐

WATER VISIBILITY

1	2	3	4	5
CLEAR ————————————— MISTY

☐ ☐ ☐ ☐ ☐

BODY OF WATER

	LAKE		OCEAN		CANAL
	SEA		RIVER		OTHER

TRIP GOALS

OCEAN/BUOY/SURF/MARINE:

STOPS	TIME OF ARRIVAL	OBSERVATIONS

ADDITIONAL NOTES

_____

_____

_____

_____

_____

	DATE:	TIME:

STARTING POINT:

DESTINATION:

DISTANCE:

DURATION:

TEAM / PADDLE PARTNER

☐	☐
☐	☐
☐	☐

GEAR / EQUIPMENT

WEATHER CONDITIONS

TEMPERATURE ____	☼	⛅	☁	🌧	❄
WIND ____	☐	☐	☐	☐	☐

WATER VISIBILITY

	1	2	3	4	5	
CLEAR						MISTY
	☐	☐	☐	☐	☐	

BODY OF WATER

☐ LAKE	☐ OCEAN	☐ CANAL
☐ SEA	☐ RIVER	☐ OTHER

TRIP GOALS

OCEAN/BUOY/SURF/MARINE:

⊘ STOPS	⊘ TIME OF ARRIVAL	📄 OBSERVATIONS

ADDITIONAL NOTES

DATE:	TIME:

STARTING POINT:

DESTINATION:

DISTANCE:

DURATION:

TEAM / PADDLE PARTNER

☐	☐
☐	☐
☐	☐

GEAR / EQUIPMENT

WEATHER CONDITIONS

TEMPERATURE _____ ☐ ☐ ☐ ☐ ☐

WIND _____ ☐ ☐ ☐ ☐ ☐

WATER VISIBILITY

1	2	3	4	5
CLEAR _____ MISTY

☐ ☐ ☐ ☐ ☐

BODY OF WATER

LAKE	OCEAN	CANAL
SEA	RIVER	OTHER

TRIP GOALS

OCEAN/BUOY/SURF/MARINE:

⊘ STOPS	⊙ TIME OF ARRIVAL	📄 OBSERVATIONS

ADDITIONAL NOTES

DATE: _____ TIME: _____

STARTING POINT: _____

DESTINATION: _____

DISTANCE: _____

DURATION: _____

TEAM / PADDLE PARTNER

☐	☐
☐	☐
☐	☐

GEAR / EQUIPMENT

WEATHER CONDITIONS

TEMPERATURE _____ ☀ ⛅ ☁ 🌧 ❄

WIND _____ ☐ ☐ ☐ ☐ ☐

WATER VISIBILITY

1	2	3	4	5
CLEAR				MISTY
☐	☐	☐	☐	☐

BODY OF WATER

	LAKE		OCEAN		CANAL
	SEA		RIVER		OTHER

TRIP GOALS

OCEAN/BUOY/SURF/MARINE: _____

⊘ STOPS	⏱ TIME OF ARRIVAL	📄 OBSERVATIONS

ADDITIONAL NOTES

_____

_____

_____

_____

	DATE:	TIME:

STARTING POINT:

DESTINATION:

DISTANCE:

DURATION:

TEAM / PADDLE PARTNER

☐	☐
☐	☐
☐	☐

GEAR / EQUIPMENT

WEATHER CONDITIONS

TEMPERATURE _____

WIND _____ ☐ ☐ ☐ ☐ ☐

WATER VISIBILITY

CLEAR 1 2 3 4 5 MISTY

☐ ☐ ☐ ☐ ☐

BODY OF WATER

LAKE	OCEAN	CANAL
SEA	RIVER	OTHER

TRIP GOALS

OCEAN/BUOY/SURF/MARINE:

STOPS	TIME OF ARRIVAL	OBSERVATIONS

ADDITIONAL NOTES

_____

_____

_____

_____

_____

DATE:	TIME:

STARTING POINT:

DESTINATION:

DISTANCE:

DURATION:

TEAM / PADDLE PARTNER

☐	☐
☐	☐
☐	☐

GEAR / EQUIPMENT

WEATHER CONDITIONS

TEMPERATURE _____ ☀ ⛅ ☁ 🌧 ❄

WIND _____ ☐ ☐ ☐ ☐ ☐

WATER VISIBILITY

	1	2	3	4	5	
CLEAR						MISTY
	☐	☐	☐	☐	☐	

BODY OF WATER

LAKE	OCEAN	CANAL
SEA	RIVER	OTHER

TRIP GOALS

OCEAN/BUOY/SURF/MARINE:

⊙ STOPS	⏱ TIME OF ARRIVAL	📄 OBSERVATIONS

ADDITIONAL NOTES

DATE: **TIME:**

STARTING POINT:

DESTINATION:

DISTANCE:

DURATION:

WEATHER CONDITIONS

TEMPERATURE ____ ☼ ⛅ ☁ 🌧 ❄

WIND ____ ☐ ☐ ☐ ☐ ☐

WATER VISIBILITY

	1	2	3	4	5	
CLEAR						MISTY
	☐	☐	☐	☐	☐	

TEAM / PADDLE PARTNER

☐	☐
☐	☐
☐	☐

BODY OF WATER

☐ LAKE	☐ OCEAN	☐ CANAL
☐ SEA	☐ RIVER	☐ OTHER

GEAR / EQUIPMENT

TRIP GOALS

OCEAN/BUOY/SURF/MARINE:

📍 STOPS	🕐 TIME OF ARRIVAL	📄 OBSERVATIONS

ADDITIONAL NOTES

	DATE:	TIME:

STARTING POINT:

DESTINATION:

DISTANCE:

DURATION:

TEAM / PADDLE PARTNER

☐	☐
☐	☐
☐	☐

GEAR / EQUIPMENT

WEATHER CONDITIONS

TEMPERATURE _____ ☀ ⛅ ☁ 🌧 ❄

WIND _____ ☐ ☐ ☐ ☐ ☐

WATER VISIBILITY

CLEAR 1   2   3   4   5 MISTY

☐   ☐   ☐   ☐   ☐

BODY OF WATER

	LAKE		OCEAN		CANAL
	SEA		RIVER		OTHER

TRIP GOALS

OCEAN/BUOY/SURF/MARINE:

⊘ STOPS	⊘ TIME OF ARRIVAL	📄 OBSERVATIONS

ADDITIONAL NOTES

📅 DATE:	TIME:

📍 **STARTING POINT:**

📍 **DESTINATION:**

🕐 **DISTANCE:**

⏱️ **DURATION:**

👥 TEAM / PADDLE PARTNER

☐	☐
☐	☐
☐	☐

GEAR / EQUIPMENT

WEATHER CONDITIONS

TEMPERATURE _____ ☀️ ⛅ ☁️ 🌧️ ❄️

WIND _____ ☐ ☐ ☐ ☐ ☐

WATER VISIBILITY

1	2	3	4	5
CLEAR				MISTY
☐	☐	☐	☐	☐

BODY OF WATER

☐ LAKE	☐ OCEAN	☐ CANAL
☐ SEA	☐ RIVER	☐ OTHER

TRIP GOALS

OCEAN/BUOY/SURF/MARINE:

📍 STOPS	🕐 TIME OF ARRIVAL	📄 OBSERVATIONS

ADDITIONAL NOTES

_____

_____

_____

_____

_____

DATE: **TIME:**

STARTING POINT:

DESTINATION:

DISTANCE:

DURATION:

TEAM / PADDLE PARTNER

☐	☐
☐	☐
☐	☐

GEAR / EQUIPMENT

WEATHER CONDITIONS

TEMPERATURE _____ ☼ ⛅ ☁ 🌧 ❄

WIND _____ ☐ ☐ ☐ ☐ ☐

WATER VISIBILITY

1	2	3	4	5
CLEAR — — — — — MISTY

☐ ☐ ☐ ☐ ☐

BODY OF WATER

☐ LAKE	☐ OCEAN	☐ CANAL
☐ SEA	☐ RIVER	☐ OTHER

TRIP GOALS

OCEAN/BUOY/SURF/MARINE:

⊙ STOPS	⊙ TIME OF ARRIVAL	▤ OBSERVATIONS

ADDITIONAL NOTES

	DATE:	TIME:

STARTING POINT:

DESTINATION:

DISTANCE:

DURATION:

TEAM / PADDLE PARTNER

☐	☐
☐	☐
☐	☐

GEAR / EQUIPMENT

WEATHER CONDITIONS

TEMPERATURE _____ ☼ ⛅ ☁ 🌧 ❄

WIND _____ ☐ ☐ ☐ ☐ ☐

WATER VISIBILITY

CLEAR	1	2	3	4	5	MISTY
	☐	☐	☐	☐	☐	

BODY OF WATER

	LAKE		OCEAN		CANAL
	SEA		RIVER		OTHER

TRIP GOALS

OCEAN/BUOY/SURF/MARINE:

⊘ STOPS	⏱ TIME OF ARRIVAL	🗎 OBSERVATIONS

ADDITIONAL NOTES

DATE: **TIME:**

STARTING POINT:

DESTINATION:

DISTANCE:

DURATION:

WEATHER CONDITIONS

TEMPERATURE _____

WIND _____ ☐ ☐ ☐ ☐ ☐

WATER VISIBILITY

CLEAR | 1   2   3   4   5 | MISTY

☐   ☐   ☐   ☐   ☐

TEAM / PADDLE PARTNER

☐	☐
☐	☐
☐	☐

BODY OF WATER

	LAKE		OCEAN		CANAL
	SEA		RIVER		OTHER

GEAR / EQUIPMENT

TRIP GOALS

OCEAN/BUOY/SURF/MARINE:

📍 STOPS	🕐 TIME OF ARRIVAL	📄 OBSERVATIONS

ADDITIONAL NOTES

	DATE:	TIME:

STARTING POINT:

DESTINATION:

DISTANCE:

DURATION:

TEAM / PADDLE PARTNER

☐	☐
☐	☐
☐	☐

GEAR / EQUIPMENT

WEATHER CONDITIONS

TEMPERATURE _____ ☀ ⛅ ☁ 🌧 ❄

WIND _____ ☐ ☐ ☐ ☐ ☐

WATER VISIBILITY

1	2	3	4	5
CLEAR ———————————————————— MISTY

☐ ☐ ☐ ☐ ☐

BODY OF WATER

LAKE	OCEAN	CANAL
SEA	RIVER	OTHER

TRIP GOALS

OCEAN/BUOY/SURF/MARINE:

📍 STOPS	🕐 TIME OF ARRIVAL	📄 OBSERVATIONS

ADDITIONAL NOTES

_____

_____

_____

_____

_____

	DATE:	TIME:

	STARTING POINT:

	DESTINATION:

	DISTANCE:

	DURATION:

WEATHER CONDITIONS

TEMPERATURE _____

WIND _____

WATER VISIBILITY

CLEAR 1 2 3 4 5 MISTY

TEAM / PADDLE PARTNER

☐	☐
☐	☐
☐	☐

BODY OF WATER

LAKE	OCEAN	CANAL
SEA	RIVER	OTHER

GEAR / EQUIPMENT

TRIP GOALS

OCEAN/BUOY/SURF/MARINE:

STOPS	TIME OF ARRIVAL	OBSERVATIONS

ADDITIONAL NOTES

📅 DATE:	TIME:

WEATHER CONDITIONS

🌡 TEMPERATURE ____ ☀ ⛅ ☁ 🌧 🌨

📶 WIND ____ ☐ ☐ ☐ ☐ ☐

WATER VISIBILITY

1	2	3	4	5

CLEAR ▭▭▭▭▭ MISTY

☐ ☐ ☐ ☐ ☐

📍 **STARTING POINT:**

✓ **DESTINATION:**

🕐 **DISTANCE:**

⏱ **DURATION:**

👥 TEAM / PADDLE PARTNER

☐	☐
☐	☐
☐	☐

BODY OF WATER

▢ LAKE	▢ OCEAN	▢ CANAL
▢ SEA	▢ RIVER	▢ OTHER

GEAR / EQUIPMENT

TRIP GOALS

OCEAN/BUOY/SURF/MARINE:

📍 STOPS	🕐 TIME OF ARRIVAL	📄 OBSERVATIONS

ADDITIONAL NOTES

_____

_____

_____

_____

_____

DATE:	TIME:

STARTING POINT:

DESTINATION:

DISTANCE:

DURATION:

WEATHER CONDITIONS

TEMPERATURE _____

WIND _____ ☐ ☐ ☐ ☐ ☐

WATER VISIBILITY

CLEAR | 1 | 2 | 3 | 4 | 5 | MISTY
☐ ☐ ☐ ☐ ☐

TEAM / PADDLE PARTNER

☐	☐
☐	☐
☐	☐

BODY OF WATER

	LAKE		OCEAN		CANAL
	SEA		RIVER		OTHER

GEAR / EQUIPMENT

TRIP GOALS

OCEAN/BUOY/SURF/MARINE:

⊘ STOPS	⊘ TIME OF ARRIVAL	▤ OBSERVATIONS

ADDITIONAL NOTES

_____

_____

_____

_____

_____

DATE: TIME:

STARTING POINT:

DESTINATION:

DISTANCE:

DURATION:

TEAM / PADDLE PARTNER

☐	☐
☐	☐
☐	☐

GEAR / EQUIPMENT

WEATHER CONDITIONS

TEMPERATURE _____ ☀ ⛅ ☁ 🌧 ❄

WIND _____ ☐ ☐ ☐ ☐ ☐

WATER VISIBILITY

CLEAR	1	2	3	4	5	MISTY
	☐	☐	☐	☐	☐	

BODY OF WATER

☐ LAKE	☐ OCEAN	☐ CANAL
☐ SEA	☐ RIVER	☐ OTHER

TRIP GOALS

OCEAN/BUOY/SURF/MARINE:

STOPS	TIME OF ARRIVAL	OBSERVATIONS

ADDITIONAL NOTES

_____
_____
_____
_____
_____

	DATE:	TIME:

	STARTING POINT:

	DESTINATION:

	DISTANCE:

	DURATION:

WEATHER CONDITIONS

TEMPERATURE _____ ☼ ⛅ ☁ 🌧 ❄

WIND _____ ☐ ☐ ☐ ☐ ☐

WATER VISIBILITY

	1	2	3	4	5	
CLEAR						MISTY
	☐	☐	☐	☐	☐	

TEAM / PADDLE PARTNER

☐	☐
☐	☐
☐	☐

BODY OF WATER

	LAKE		OCEAN		CANAL
	SEA		RIVER		OTHER

GEAR / EQUIPMENT

TRIP GOALS

OCEAN/BUOY/SURF/MARINE:

⊘ STOPS	🕐 TIME OF ARRIVAL	📄 OBSERVATIONS

ADDITIONAL NOTES

DATE:	TIME:

STARTING POINT:

DESTINATION:

DISTANCE:

DURATION:

TEAM / PADDLE PARTNER

☐	☐
☐	☐
☐	☐

GEAR / EQUIPMENT

WEATHER CONDITIONS

TEMPERATURE	___	☀	⛅	☁	🌧	❄
WIND	___	☐	☐	☐	☐	☐

WATER VISIBILITY

	1	2	3	4	5	
CLEAR						MISTY
	☐	☐	☐	☐	☐	

BODY OF WATER

	LAKE		OCEAN		CANAL
	SEA		RIVER		OTHER

TRIP GOALS

OCEAN/BUOY/SURF/MARINE:

⊘ STOPS	⊘ TIME OF ARRIVAL	🗎 OBSERVATIONS

ADDITIONAL NOTES

DATE: TIME:

STARTING POINT:

DESTINATION:

DISTANCE:

DURATION:

TEAM / PADDLE PARTNER

☐	☐
☐	☐
☐	☐

GEAR / EQUIPMENT

WEATHER CONDITIONS

TEMPERATURE _____

WIND _____ ☐ ☐ ☐ ☐ ☐

WATER VISIBILITY

CLEAR   1   2   3   4   5   MISTY

☐ ☐ ☐ ☐ ☐

BODY OF WATER

LAKE	OCEAN	CANAL
SEA	RIVER	OTHER

TRIP GOALS

OCEAN/BUOY/SURF/MARINE:

⊙ STOPS	⏱ TIME OF ARRIVAL	🗎 OBSERVATIONS

ADDITIONAL NOTES

DATE:	TIME:

STARTING POINT:

DESTINATION:

DISTANCE:

DURATION:

WEATHER CONDITIONS

TEMPERATURE _____ ☼ ⛅ ☁ 🌧 ❄

WIND _____ ☐ ☐ ☐ ☐ ☐

WATER VISIBILITY

CLEAR | 1 | 2 | 3 | 4 | 5 | MISTY

☐ ☐ ☐ ☐ ☐

TEAM / PADDLE PARTNER

☐	☐
☐	☐
☐	☐

BODY OF WATER

	LAKE		OCEAN		CANAL
	SEA		RIVER		OTHER

GEAR / EQUIPMENT

TRIP GOALS

OCEAN/BUOY/SURF/MARINE:

⊘ STOPS	⊙ TIME OF ARRIVAL	📄 OBSERVATIONS

ADDITIONAL NOTES

	DATE:	TIME:

STARTING POINT:

DESTINATION:

DISTANCE:

DURATION:

TEAM / PADDLE PARTNER

☐	☐
☐	☐
☐	☐

GEAR / EQUIPMENT

WEATHER CONDITIONS

TEMPERATURE _____ ☀ ⛅ ☁ 🌧 ❄

WIND _____ ☐ ☐ ☐ ☐ ☐

WATER VISIBILITY

	1	2	3	4	5	
CLEAR						MISTY

☐ ☐ ☐ ☐ ☐

BODY OF WATER

	LAKE		OCEAN		CANAL
	SEA		RIVER		OTHER

TRIP GOALS

OCEAN/BUOY/SURF/MARINE:

⊘ STOPS	🕐 TIME OF ARRIVAL	📄 OBSERVATIONS

ADDITIONAL NOTES

📅 DATE:	TIME:

📍 STARTING POINT:

✅ DESTINATION:

🕐 DISTANCE:

⏱ DURATION:

WEATHER CONDITIONS

🌡 TEMPERATURE ____ ☀ ⛅ ☁ 🌧 ❄

|||| WIND ____ ☐ ☐ ☐ ☐ ☐

WATER VISIBILITY

CLEAR	1	2	3	4	5	MISTY
	☐	☐	☐	☐	☐	

👥 TEAM / PADDLE PARTNER

☐	☐
☐	☐
☐	☐

BODY OF WATER

▢ LAKE	▢ OCEAN	▢ CANAL
▢ SEA	▢ RIVER	▢ OTHER

GEAR / EQUIPMENT

TRIP GOALS

OCEAN/BUOY/SURF/MARINE:

📍 STOPS	🕐 TIME OF ARRIVAL	📄 OBSERVATIONS

ADDITIONAL NOTES

📅 DATE: TIME:	

📍 STARTING POINT:

📍 DESTINATION:

🕐 DISTANCE:

⏱ DURATION:

WEATHER CONDITIONS

🌡 TEMPERATURE _____ ☀ ⛅ ☁ 🌧 ❄

🌡 WIND _____ ☐ ☐ ☐ ☐ ☐

WATER VISIBILITY

CLEAR | 1 | 2 | 3 | 4 | 5 | MISTY

☐ ☐ ☐ ☐ ☐

👥 TEAM / PADDLE PARTNER

☐	☐
☐	☐
☐	☐

BODY OF WATER

	LAKE		OCEAN		CANAL
	SEA		RIVER		OTHER

GEAR / EQUIPMENT

TRIP GOALS

OCEAN/BUOY/SURF/MARINE:

📍 STOPS	🕐 TIME OF ARRIVAL	📄 OBSERVATIONS

ADDITIONAL NOTES

DATE: TIME:

STARTING POINT:

DESTINATION:

DISTANCE:

DURATION:

TEAM / PADDLE PARTNER

☐	☐
☐	☐
☐	☐

GEAR / EQUIPMENT

WEATHER CONDITIONS

TEMPERATURE _____ ☼ ⛅ ☁ 🌦 ❄

WIND _____ ☐ ☐ ☐ ☐ ☐

WATER VISIBILITY

CLEAR	1	2	3	4	5	MISTY
	☐	☐	☐	☐	☐	

BODY OF WATER

	LAKE		OCEAN		CANAL
	SEA		RIVER		OTHER

TRIP GOALS

OCEAN/BUOY/SURF/MARINE:

📍 STOPS	⏱ TIME OF ARRIVAL	📄 OBSERVATIONS

ADDITIONAL NOTES

_____

_____

_____

_____

_____

📅 DATE:	TIME:
📍 STARTING POINT:	
🏷️ DESTINATION:	
🕐 DISTANCE:	
⏱️ DURATION:	

WEATHER CONDITIONS

🌡️ TEMPERATURE _____ ☀️ ⛅ ☁️ 🌧️ ❄️

💨 WIND _____ ☐ ☐ ☐ ☐ ☐

WATER VISIBILITY

CLEAR | 1   2   3   4   5 | MISTY

☐ ☐ ☐ ☐ ☐

👥 TEAM / PADDLE PARTNER

☐	☐
☐	☐
☐	☐

BODY OF WATER

☐ LAKE	☐ OCEAN	☐ CANAL
☐ SEA	☐ RIVER	☐ OTHER

GEAR / EQUIPMENT

TRIP GOALS

OCEAN/BUOY/SURF/MARINE:

📍 STOPS	🕐 TIME OF ARRIVAL	📄 OBSERVATIONS

ADDITIONAL NOTES

| 📅 DATE: | TIME: |

| 📍 STARTING POINT: |

| 📍 DESTINATION: |

| 🕐 DISTANCE: |

| ⏱ DURATION: |

WEATHER CONDITIONS

🌡 TEMPERATURE _____ ☀ ⛅ ☁ 🌧 ❄

💨 WIND _____ ☐ ☐ ☐ ☐ ☐

WATER VISIBILITY

CLEAR | 1 | 2 | 3 | 4 | 5 | MISTY
☐ ☐ ☐ ☐ ☐

👥 TEAM / PADDLE PARTNER

☐	☐
☐	☐
☐	☐

BODY OF WATER

| ☐ LAKE | ☐ OCEAN | ☐ CANAL |
| ☐ SEA | ☐ RIVER | ☐ OTHER |

GEAR / EQUIPMENT

TRIP GOALS

OCEAN/BUOY/SURF/MARINE:

📍 STOPS	🕐 TIME OF ARRIVAL	📄 OBSERVATIONS

ADDITIONAL NOTES

DATE:	TIME:

STARTING POINT:

DESTINATION:

DISTANCE:

DURATION:

TEAM / PADDLE PARTNER

☐	☐
☐	☐
☐	☐

GEAR / EQUIPMENT

WEATHER CONDITIONS

TEMPERATURE _____ ☀ ⛅ ☁ 🌧 ❄

WIND _____ ☐ ☐ ☐ ☐ ☐

WATER VISIBILITY

1	2	3	4	5
CLEAR ████████████ MISTY

☐ ☐ ☐ ☐ ☐

BODY OF WATER

	LAKE		OCEAN		CANAL
	SEA		RIVER		OTHER

TRIP GOALS

OCEAN/BUOY/SURF/MARINE:

📍 STOPS	🕐 TIME OF ARRIVAL	📄 OBSERVATIONS

ADDITIONAL NOTES

DATE: TIME:

STARTING POINT:

DESTINATION:

DISTANCE:

DURATION:

TEAM / PADDLE PARTNER

☐	☐
☐	☐
☐	☐

GEAR / EQUIPMENT

WEATHER CONDITIONS

TEMPERATURE _____ ☀ ⛅ ☁ 🌧 ❄

WIND _____ ☐ ☐ ☐ ☐ ☐

WATER VISIBILITY

CLEAR   1   2   3   4   5   MISTY

☐   ☐   ☐   ☐   ☐

BODY OF WATER

LAKE	OCEAN	CANAL
SEA	RIVER	OTHER

TRIP GOALS

OCEAN/BUOY/SURF/MARINE:

⊘ STOPS	⊙ TIME OF ARRIVAL	🗎 OBSERVATIONS

ADDITIONAL NOTES

_____

_____

_____

_____

_____

_____

📅 DATE: _____ TIME: _____

📍 STARTING POINT: _____

📍 DESTINATION: _____

🕐 DISTANCE: _____

⏱ DURATION: _____

👥 TEAM / PADDLE PARTNER

☐	☐
☐	☐
☐	☐

GEAR / EQUIPMENT

WEATHER CONDITIONS

🌡 TEMPERATURE ____ ☀ 🌤 ☁ 🌧 ❄

〰 WIND ____ ☐ ☐ ☐ ☐ ☐

WATER VISIBILITY

1	2	3	4	5
CLEAR				MISTY
☐	☐	☐	☐	☐

BODY OF WATER

☐ LAKE	☐ OCEAN	☐ CANAL
☐ SEA	☐ RIVER	☐ OTHER

TRIP GOALS

OCEAN/BUOY/SURF/MARINE: _____

📍 STOPS	🕐 TIME OF ARRIVAL	📄 OBSERVATIONS

ADDITIONAL NOTES

_____

_____

_____

_____

_____

DATE: TIME:

STARTING POINT:

DESTINATION:

DISTANCE:

DURATION:

TEAM / PADDLE PARTNER

☐	☐
☐	☐
☐	☐

GEAR / EQUIPMENT

WEATHER CONDITIONS

TEMPERATURE _____	☀	⛅	☁	🌧	❄
WIND _____	☐	☐	☐	☐	☐

WATER VISIBILITY

CLEAR   1   2   3   4   5   MISTY

☐   ☐   ☐   ☐   ☐

BODY OF WATER

☐ LAKE	☐ OCEAN	☐ CANAL
☐ SEA	☐ RIVER	☐ OTHER

TRIP GOALS

OCEAN/BUOY/SURF/MARINE:

⦿ STOPS	⌚ TIME OF ARRIVAL	🗎 OBSERVATIONS

ADDITIONAL NOTES

DATE:	TIME:

STARTING POINT:

DESTINATION:

DISTANCE:

DURATION:

WEATHER CONDITIONS

TEMPERATURE _____ ☀ ⛅ ☁ 🌧 ❄

WIND _____ ☐ ☐ ☐ ☐ ☐

WATER VISIBILITY

	1	2	3	4	5	
CLEAR						MISTY
	☐	☐	☐	☐	☐	

TEAM / PADDLE PARTNER

☐	☐
☐	☐
☐	☐

BODY OF WATER

	LAKE		OCEAN		CANAL
	SEA		RIVER		OTHER

GEAR / EQUIPMENT

TRIP GOALS

OCEAN/BUOY/SURF/MARINE:

STOPS	TIME OF ARRIVAL	OBSERVATIONS

ADDITIONAL NOTES

	DATE:	TIME:

STARTING POINT:

DESTINATION:

DISTANCE:

DURATION:

TEAM / PADDLE PARTNER

☐	☐
☐	☐
☐	☐

GEAR / EQUIPMENT

WEATHER CONDITIONS

TEMPERATURE ____	☀	⛅	☁	🌧	❄
WIND ____	☐	☐	☐	☐	☐

WATER VISIBILITY

CLEAR | 1 | 2 | 3 | 4 | 5 | MISTY

☐ ☐ ☐ ☐ ☐

BODY OF WATER

☐ LAKE	☐ OCEAN	☐ CANAL
☐ SEA	☐ RIVER	☐ OTHER

TRIP GOALS

OCEAN/BUOY/SURF/MARINE:

⊘ STOPS	⏱ TIME OF ARRIVAL	📄 OBSERVATIONS

ADDITIONAL NOTES

_____

_____

_____

_____

_____

_____

📅 DATE: TIME:	**WEATHER CONDITIONS**
📍 STARTING POINT:	🌡️ TEMPERATURE ____ ☀️ ⛅ ☁️ 🌧️ ❄️
📍 DESTINATION:	💨 WIND ____ ☐ ☐ ☐ ☐ ☐

WEATHER CONDITIONS

🌡️ TEMPERATURE _____ ☀️ ⛅ ☁️ 🌧️ ❄️

💨 WIND _____ ☐ ☐ ☐ ☐ ☐

WATER VISIBILITY

CLEAR | 1   2   3   4   5 | MISTY

☐   ☐   ☐   ☐   ☐

📅 DATE: TIME:

📍 STARTING POINT:

📍 DESTINATION:

🕐 DISTANCE:

⏱️ DURATION:

👥 TEAM / PADDLE PARTNER

☐	☐
☐	☐
☐	☐

GEAR / EQUIPMENT

BODY OF WATER

☐ LAKE	☐ OCEAN	☐ CANAL
☐ SEA	☐ RIVER	☐ OTHER

TRIP GOALS

OCEAN/BUOY/SURF/MARINE:

📍 STOPS	🕐 TIME OF ARRIVAL	📄 OBSERVATIONS

ADDITIONAL NOTES

	DATE:	TIME:

	STARTING POINT:

	DESTINATION:

	DISTANCE:

	DURATION:

WEATHER CONDITIONS

TEMPERATURE _____ ☼ ⛅ ☁ 🌧 ❄

WIND _____ ☐ ☐ ☐ ☐ ☐

WATER VISIBILITY

	1	2	3	4	5	
CLEAR						MISTY
	☐	☐	☐	☐	☐	

TEAM / PADDLE PARTNER

☐	☐
☐	☐
☐	☐

BODY OF WATER

LAKE	OCEAN	CANAL
SEA	RIVER	OTHER

GEAR / EQUIPMENT

TRIP GOALS

OCEAN/BUOY/SURF/MARINE:

STOPS	TIME OF ARRIVAL	OBSERVATIONS

ADDITIONAL NOTES

_____

_____

_____

_____

_____

DATE:	TIME:

STARTING POINT:

DESTINATION:

DISTANCE:

DURATION:

WEATHER CONDITIONS

TEMPERATURE _____ ☀ ⛅ ☁ 🌧 ❄

WIND _____ ☐ ☐ ☐ ☐ ☐

WATER VISIBILITY

CLEAR |____1____2____3____4____5____| MISTY

☐ ☐ ☐ ☐ ☐

TEAM / PADDLE PARTNER

☐	☐
☐	☐
☐	☐

BODY OF WATER

☐ LAKE	☐ OCEAN	☐ CANAL
☐ SEA	☐ RIVER	☐ OTHER

GEAR / EQUIPMENT

TRIP GOALS

OCEAN/BUOY/SURF/MARINE:

📍 STOPS	🕐 TIME OF ARRIVAL	📄 OBSERVATIONS

ADDITIONAL NOTES

DATE: TIME:

STARTING POINT:

DESTINATION:

DISTANCE:

DURATION:

TEAM / PADDLE PARTNER

☐	☐
☐	☐
☐	☐

GEAR / EQUIPMENT

WEATHER CONDITIONS

TEMPERATURE _____ ☀ ⛅ ☁ 🌧 ❄

WIND _____ ☐ ☐ ☐ ☐ ☐

WATER VISIBILITY

CLEAR 1 2 3 4 5 MISTY

☐ ☐ ☐ ☐ ☐

BODY OF WATER

LAKE	OCEAN	CANAL
SEA	RIVER	OTHER

TRIP GOALS

OCEAN/BUOY/SURF/MARINE:

⊘ STOPS	⊙ TIME OF ARRIVAL	📄 OBSERVATIONS

ADDITIONAL NOTES

DATE: TIME:

STARTING POINT:

DESTINATION:

DISTANCE:

DURATION:

TEAM / PADDLE PARTNER

☐	☐
☐	☐
☐	☐

GEAR / EQUIPMENT

WEATHER CONDITIONS

TEMPERATURE ____ ☐ ☐ ☐ ☐ ☐

WIND ____

WATER VISIBILITY

CLEAR | 1 | 2 | 3 | 4 | 5 | MISTY

☐ ☐ ☐ ☐ ☐

BODY OF WATER

☐ LAKE	☐ OCEAN	☐ CANAL
☐ SEA	☐ RIVER	☐ OTHER

TRIP GOALS

OCEAN/BUOY/SURF/MARINE:

⊘ STOPS	⏱ TIME OF ARRIVAL	📄 OBSERVATIONS

ADDITIONAL NOTES

📅 DATE:	TIME:

📍 STARTING POINT:

✅ DESTINATION:

🕐 DISTANCE:

⏱ DURATION:

WEATHER CONDITIONS

🌡 TEMPERATURE ____ ☀ ⛅ ☁ 🌧 ❄

💨 WIND ____ ☐ ☐ ☐ ☐ ☐

WATER VISIBILITY

	1	2	3	4	5	
CLEAR						MISTY
	☐	☐	☐	☐	☐	

👥 TEAM / PADDLE PARTNER

☐	☐
☐	☐
☐	☐

BODY OF WATER

LAKE	OCEAN	CANAL
SEA	RIVER	OTHER

GEAR / EQUIPMENT

TRIP GOALS

OCEAN/BUOY/SURF/MARINE:

✅ STOPS	🕐 TIME OF ARRIVAL	📄 OBSERVATIONS

ADDITIONAL NOTES

DATE: **TIME:**

STARTING POINT:

DESTINATION:

DISTANCE:

DURATION:

WEATHER CONDITIONS

TEMPERATURE _____

WIND _____

WATER VISIBILITY

CLEAR | 1 | 2 | 3 | 4 | 5 | MISTY

TEAM / PADDLE PARTNER

☐	☐
☐	☐
☐	☐

BODY OF WATER

	LAKE		OCEAN		CANAL
	SEA		RIVER		OTHER

GEAR / EQUIPMENT

TRIP GOALS

OCEAN/BUOY/SURF/MARINE:

⊘ STOPS	⏱ TIME OF ARRIVAL	📄 OBSERVATIONS

ADDITIONAL NOTES

DATE: TIME:

STARTING POINT:

DESTINATION:

DISTANCE:

DURATION:

TEAM / PADDLE PARTNER

☐	☐
☐	☐
☐	☐

GEAR / EQUIPMENT

WEATHER CONDITIONS

TEMPERATURE _____ ☼ ⛅ ☁ 🌧 ❄

WIND _____ ☐ ☐ ☐ ☐ ☐

WATER VISIBILITY

1	2	3	4	5
CLEAR ☐ ☐ ☐ ☐ ☐ MISTY

BODY OF WATER

LAKE	OCEAN	CANAL
SEA	RIVER	OTHER

TRIP GOALS

OCEAN/BUOY/SURF/MARINE:

⚲ STOPS	⊘ TIME OF ARRIVAL	🗎 OBSERVATIONS

ADDITIONAL NOTES

_____
_____
_____
_____
_____

DATE:	TIME:

STARTING POINT:

DESTINATION:

DISTANCE:

DURATION:

TEAM / PADDLE PARTNER

☐	☐
☐	☐
☐	☐

GEAR / EQUIPMENT

WEATHER CONDITIONS

TEMPERATURE _____ ☀ ⛅ ☁ 🌧 ❄

WIND _____ ☐ ☐ ☐ ☐ ☐

WATER VISIBILITY

	1	2	3	4	5	
CLEAR						MISTY

☐ ☐ ☐ ☐ ☐

BODY OF WATER

	LAKE		OCEAN		CANAL
	SEA		RIVER		OTHER

TRIP GOALS

OCEAN/BUOY/SURF/MARINE:

⊘ STOPS	⊙ TIME OF ARRIVAL	📄 OBSERVATIONS

ADDITIONAL NOTES

	DATE:	TIME:

STARTING POINT:

DESTINATION:

DISTANCE:

DURATION:

TEAM / PADDLE PARTNER

☐	☐
☐	☐
☐	☐

GEAR / EQUIPMENT

WEATHER CONDITIONS

TEMPERATURE _____ ☀ ⛅ ☁ 🌧 ❄

WIND _____ ☐ ☐ ☐ ☐ ☐

WATER VISIBILITY

	1	2	3	4	5	
CLEAR						MISTY
	☐	☐	☐	☐	☐	

BODY OF WATER

☐ LAKE	☐ OCEAN	☐ CANAL
☐ SEA	☐ RIVER	☐ OTHER

TRIP GOALS

OCEAN/BUOY/SURF/MARINE:

📍 STOPS	🕐 TIME OF ARRIVAL	📄 OBSERVATIONS

ADDITIONAL NOTES

DATE:	TIME:

STARTING POINT:

DESTINATION:

DISTANCE:

DURATION:

WEATHER CONDITIONS

TEMPERATURE ____ ☼ ⛅ ☁ 🌧 ❄

WIND ____ ☐ ☐ ☐ ☐ ☐

WATER VISIBILITY

	1	2	3	4	5	
CLEAR						MISTY
	☐	☐	☐	☐	☐	

TEAM / PADDLE PARTNER

☐	☐
☐	☐
☐	☐

BODY OF WATER

☐ LAKE	☐ OCEAN	☐ CANAL
☐ SEA	☐ RIVER	☐ OTHER

GEAR / EQUIPMENT

TRIP GOALS

OCEAN/BUOY/SURF/MARINE:

⦿ STOPS	⦿ TIME OF ARRIVAL	🗎 OBSERVATIONS

ADDITIONAL NOTES

	DATE:		TIME:

STARTING POINT:

DESTINATION:

DISTANCE:

DURATION:

TEAM / PADDLE PARTNER

☐	☐
☐	☐
☐	☐

GEAR / EQUIPMENT

WEATHER CONDITIONS

TEMPERATURE _____ ☀ ⛅ ☁ 🌧 ❄

WIND _____ ☐ ☐ ☐ ☐ ☐

WATER VISIBILITY

1	2	3	4	5
CLEAR				MISTY
☐	☐	☐	☐	☐

BODY OF WATER

LAKE	OCEAN	CANAL
SEA	RIVER	OTHER

TRIP GOALS

OCEAN/BUOY/SURF/MARINE:

⊘ STOPS	⊙ TIME OF ARRIVAL	▤ OBSERVATIONS

ADDITIONAL NOTES

	DATE:	TIME:

WEATHER CONDITIONS

TEMPERATURE _____

WIND _____

WATER VISIBILITY

CLEAR | 1 | 2 | 3 | 4 | 5 | MISTY

STARTING POINT:

DESTINATION:

DISTANCE:

DURATION:

TEAM / PADDLE PARTNER

☐	☐
☐	☐
☐	☐

BODY OF WATER

	LAKE		OCEAN		CANAL
	SEA		RIVER		OTHER

GEAR / EQUIPMENT

TRIP GOALS

OCEAN/BUOY/SURF/MARINE:

STOPS	TIME OF ARRIVAL	OBSERVATIONS

ADDITIONAL NOTES

	DATE:	TIME:

STARTING POINT:

DESTINATION:

DISTANCE:

DURATION:

TEAM / PADDLE PARTNER

☐	☐
☐	☐
☐	☐

GEAR / EQUIPMENT

WEATHER CONDITIONS

TEMPERATURE _____ ☼ ⛅ ☁ 🌧 ❄

WIND _____ ☐ ☐ ☐ ☐ ☐

WATER VISIBILITY

CLEAR | 1   2   3   4   5 | MISTY

☐ ☐ ☐ ☐ ☐

BODY OF WATER

☐ LAKE	☐ OCEAN	☐ CANAL
☐ SEA	☐ RIVER	☐ OTHER

TRIP GOALS

OCEAN/BUOY/SURF/MARINE:

⊘ STOPS	⏱ TIME OF ARRIVAL	📄 OBSERVATIONS

ADDITIONAL NOTES

📆 DATE:	TIME:

📍 **STARTING POINT:**

☑ **DESTINATION:**

🕐 **DISTANCE:**

⏱ **DURATION:**

WEATHER CONDITIONS

🌡 TEMPERATURE _____ ☀ ⛅ ☁ 🌧 ❄

WIND _____ ☐ ☐ ☐ ☐ ☐

WATER VISIBILITY

CLEAR |1   2   3   4   5| MISTY
☐   ☐   ☐   ☐   ☐

TEAM / PADDLE PARTNER

☐	☐
☐	☐
☐	☐

BODY OF WATER

☐ LAKE	☐ OCEAN	☐ CANAL
☐ SEA	☐ RIVER	☐ OTHER

GEAR / EQUIPMENT

TRIP GOALS

OCEAN/BUOY/SURF/MARINE:

📍 STOPS	🕐 TIME OF ARRIVAL	📄 OBSERVATIONS

ADDITIONAL NOTES

📅 DATE:	TIME:

📍 STARTING POINT:

📍 DESTINATION:

🕐 DISTANCE:

⏱ DURATION:

👥 TEAM / PADDLE PARTNER

☐	☐
☐	☐
☐	☐

GEAR / EQUIPMENT

WEATHER CONDITIONS

🌡 TEMPERATURE _____	☀	⛅	☁	🌧	❄
WIND _____	☐	☐	☐	☐	☐

WATER VISIBILITY

CLEAR	1	2	3	4	5	MISTY
	☐	☐	☐	☐	☐	

BODY OF WATER

▢ LAKE	▢ OCEAN	▢ CANAL
▢ SEA	▢ RIVER	▢ OTHER

TRIP GOALS

OCEAN/BUOY/SURF/MARINE:

📍 STOPS	🕐 TIME OF ARRIVAL	📄 OBSERVATIONS

ADDITIONAL NOTES

_____

_____

_____

_____

_____

	DATE:	TIME:

STARTING POINT:

DESTINATION:

DISTANCE:

DURATION:

TEAM / PADDLE PARTNER

☐	☐
☐	☐
☐	☐

GEAR / EQUIPMENT

WEATHER CONDITIONS

TEMPERATURE ____	☀	⛅	☁	🌧	❄
WIND ____	☐	☐	☐	☐	☐

WATER VISIBILITY

	1	2	3	4	5	
CLEAR						MISTY
	☐	☐	☐	☐	☐	

BODY OF WATER

	LAKE		OCEAN		CANAL
	SEA		RIVER		OTHER

TRIP GOALS

OCEAN/BUOY/SURF/MARINE:

⊘ STOPS	⊙ TIME OF ARRIVAL	🗎 OBSERVATIONS

ADDITIONAL NOTES

	DATE:	TIME:

STARTING POINT:

DESTINATION:

DISTANCE:

DURATION:

WEATHER CONDITIONS

TEMPERATURE ____ ☀ ⛅ ☁ 🌧 🌧 ❄

WIND ____ ☐ ☐ ☐ ☐ ☐

WATER VISIBILITY

	1	2	3	4	5	
CLEAR						MISTY
	☐	☐	☐	☐	☐	

TEAM / PADDLE PARTNER

☐	☐
☐	☐
☐	☐

BODY OF WATER

	LAKE		OCEAN		CANAL
	SEA		RIVER		OTHER

GEAR / EQUIPMENT

TRIP GOALS

OCEAN/BUOY/SURF/MARINE:

⊘ STOPS	⊙ TIME OF ARRIVAL	🗎 OBSERVATIONS

ADDITIONAL NOTES

DATE: TIME:

STARTING POINT:

DESTINATION:

DISTANCE:

DURATION:

TEAM / PADDLE PARTNER

☐	☐
☐	☐
☐	☐

GEAR / EQUIPMENT

WEATHER CONDITIONS

TEMPERATURE _____ ☀ ⛅ ☁ 🌧 ❄

WIND _____ ☐ ☐ ☐ ☐ ☐

WATER VISIBILITY

CLEAR | 1 2 3 4 5 | MISTY

☐ ☐ ☐ ☐ ☐

BODY OF WATER

▢ LAKE	▢ OCEAN	▢ CANAL
▢ SEA	▢ RIVER	▢ OTHER

TRIP GOALS

OCEAN/BUOY/SURF/MARINE:

📍 STOPS	🕐 TIME OF ARRIVAL	📄 OBSERVATIONS

ADDITIONAL NOTES

DATE:	TIME:

STARTING POINT:

DESTINATION:

DISTANCE:

DURATION:

TEAM / PADDLE PARTNER

☐	☐
☐	☐
☐	☐

GEAR / EQUIPMENT

WEATHER CONDITIONS

TEMPERATURE _____ ☼ ⛅ ☁ 🌧 ❄

WIND _____ ☐ ☐ ☐ ☐ ☐

WATER VISIBILITY

	1	2	3	4	5	
CLEAR						MISTY
	☐	☐	☐	☐	☐	

BODY OF WATER

☐ LAKE	☐ OCEAN	☐ CANAL
☐ SEA	☐ RIVER	☐ OTHER

TRIP GOALS

OCEAN/BUOY/SURF/MARINE:

📍 STOPS	🕐 TIME OF ARRIVAL	📄 OBSERVATIONS

ADDITIONAL NOTES

DATE: **TIME:**

STARTING POINT:

DESTINATION:

DISTANCE:

DURATION:

TEAM / PADDLE PARTNER

☐	☐
☐	☐
☐	☐

GEAR / EQUIPMENT

WEATHER CONDITIONS

TEMPERATURE _____	☼ ⛅ ☁ 🌧 ❄
WIND _____	☐ ☐ ☐ ☐ ☐

WATER VISIBILITY

1	2	3	4	5
CLEAR				MISTY
☐	☐	☐	☐	☐

BODY OF WATER

☐ LAKE	☐ OCEAN	☐ CANAL
☐ SEA	☐ RIVER	☐ OTHER

TRIP GOALS

OCEAN/BUOY/SURF/MARINE:

⚲ STOPS	⏱ TIME OF ARRIVAL	🗋 OBSERVATIONS

ADDITIONAL NOTES

DATE: TIME:

STARTING POINT:

DESTINATION:

DISTANCE:

DURATION:

WEATHER CONDITIONS

TEMPERATURE _____

WIND _____

WATER VISIBILITY

| CLEAR | 1 | 2 | 3 | 4 | 5 | MISTY |

TEAM / PADDLE PARTNER

☐	☐
☐	☐
☐	☐

BODY OF WATER

	LAKE		OCEAN		CANAL
	SEA		RIVER		OTHER

GEAR / EQUIPMENT

TRIP GOALS

OCEAN/BUOY/SURF/MARINE:

⊘ STOPS	⟳ TIME OF ARRIVAL	🖹 OBSERVATIONS

ADDITIONAL NOTES

📅 DATE:	TIME:

📍 **STARTING POINT:**

📍 **DESTINATION:**

🕐 **DISTANCE:**

⏱ **DURATION:**

👥 TEAM / PADDLE PARTNER

☐	☐
☐	☐
☐	☐

GEAR / EQUIPMENT

WEATHER CONDITIONS

🌡 TEMPERATURE ____ ☀ ⛅ 🌧 🌧 ❄

🌡 WIND ____ ☐ ☐ ☐ ☐ ☐

WATER VISIBILITY

	1	2	3	4	5	
CLEAR						MISTY
	☐	☐	☐	☐	☐	

BODY OF WATER

▢ LAKE	▢ OCEAN	▢ CANAL
▢ SEA	▢ RIVER	▢ OTHER

TRIP GOALS

OCEAN/BUOY/SURF/MARINE:

📍 STOPS	🕐 TIME OF ARRIVAL	📄 OBSERVATIONS

ADDITIONAL NOTES

_____

_____

_____

_____

_____

_____

DATE: TIME:

STARTING POINT:

DESTINATION:

DISTANCE:

DURATION:

TEAM / PADDLE PARTNER

☐	☐
☐	☐
☐	☐

GEAR / EQUIPMENT

WEATHER CONDITIONS

TEMPERATURE _____ ☀ ⛅ ☁ 🌧 ❄

WIND _____ ☐ ☐ ☐ ☐ ☐

WATER VISIBILITY

	1	2	3	4	5	
CLEAR						MISTY
	☐	☐	☐	☐	☐	

BODY OF WATER

	LAKE		OCEAN		CANAL
	SEA		RIVER		OTHER

TRIP GOALS

OCEAN/BUOY/SURF/MARINE:

⊘ STOPS	🕐 TIME OF ARRIVAL	📄 OBSERVATIONS

ADDITIONAL NOTES

DATE:	TIME:

STARTING POINT:

DESTINATION:

DISTANCE:

DURATION:

TEAM / PADDLE PARTNER

☐	☐
☐	☐
☐	☐

GEAR / EQUIPMENT

WEATHER CONDITIONS

TEMPERATURE ____

WIND ____ ☐ ☐ ☐ ☐ ☐

WATER VISIBILITY

CLEAR | 1 | 2 | 3 | 4 | 5 | MISTY

☐ ☐ ☐ ☐ ☐

BODY OF WATER

LAKE	OCEAN	CANAL
SEA	RIVER	OTHER

TRIP GOALS

OCEAN/BUOY/SURF/MARINE:

📍 STOPS	🕐 TIME OF ARRIVAL	📄 OBSERVATIONS

ADDITIONAL NOTES

📅 DATE:	TIME:

📍 **STARTING POINT:**

✅ **DESTINATION:**

🕐 **DISTANCE:**

⏱ **DURATION:**

WEATHER CONDITIONS

🌡 TEMPERATURE ____   ☀ ⛅ ☁ 🌧 ❄

WIND ____ ☐ ☐ ☐ ☐ ☐

WATER VISIBILITY

	1	2	3	4	5	
CLEAR						MISTY
	☐	☐	☐	☐	☐	

👥 TEAM / PADDLE PARTNER

☐	☐
☐	☐
☐	☐

BODY OF WATER

☐ LAKE	☐ OCEAN	☐ CANAL
☐ SEA	☐ RIVER	☐ OTHER

GEAR / EQUIPMENT

TRIP GOALS

OCEAN/BUOY/SURF/MARINE:

📍 STOPS	🕐 TIME OF ARRIVAL	📄 OBSERVATIONS

ADDITIONAL NOTES

DATE: _____ **TIME:** _____

STARTING POINT: _____

DESTINATION: _____

DISTANCE: _____

DURATION: _____

TEAM / PADDLE PARTNER

☐	☐
☐	☐
☐	☐

GEAR / EQUIPMENT

WEATHER CONDITIONS

TEMPERATURE _____ ☀ ⛅ ☁ 🌧 ❄

WIND _____ ☐ ☐ ☐ ☐ ☐

WATER VISIBILITY

	1	2	3	4	5	
CLEAR						MISTY
	☐	☐	☐	☐	☐	

BODY OF WATER

☐ LAKE	☐ OCEAN	☐ CANAL
☐ SEA	☐ RIVER	☐ OTHER

TRIP GOALS

OCEAN/BUOY/SURF/MARINE: _____

⊘ STOPS	⊘ TIME OF ARRIVAL	▤ OBSERVATIONS

ADDITIONAL NOTES

_____

_____

_____

_____

_____

DATE: **TIME:**

STARTING POINT:

DESTINATION:

DISTANCE:

DURATION:

TEAM / PADDLE PARTNER

☐	☐
☐	☐
☐	☐

GEAR / EQUIPMENT

WEATHER CONDITIONS

TEMPERATURE ____ ☀ ⛅ ☁ 🌧 ❄

WIND ____ ☐ ☐ ☐ ☐ ☐

WATER VISIBILITY

CLEAR   1   2   3   4   5   MISTY

☐   ☐   ☐   ☐   ☐

BODY OF WATER

	LAKE		OCEAN		CANAL
	SEA		RIVER		OTHER

TRIP GOALS

OCEAN/BUOY/SURF/MARINE:

📍 STOPS	🕐 TIME OF ARRIVAL	📄 OBSERVATIONS

ADDITIONAL NOTES

	DATE:	TIME:

DATE: TIME:

STARTING POINT:

DESTINATION:

DISTANCE:

DURATION:

TEAM / PADDLE PARTNER

☐	☐
☐	☐
☐	☐

GEAR / EQUIPMENT

WEATHER CONDITIONS

TEMPERATURE ___	☼	⛅	☁	🌧	❄
WIND ___	☐	☐	☐	☐	☐

WATER VISIBILITY

	1	2	3	4	5	
CLEAR						MISTY
	☐	☐	☐	☐	☐	

BODY OF WATER

	LAKE		OCEAN		CANAL
	SEA		RIVER		OTHER

TRIP GOALS

OCEAN/BUOY/SURF/MARINE:

⊘ STOPS	⊘ TIME OF ARRIVAL	🗎 OBSERVATIONS

ADDITIONAL NOTES

	DATE:	TIME:

STARTING POINT:

DESTINATION:

DISTANCE:

DURATION:

WEATHER CONDITIONS

TEMPERATURE _____

WIND _____ ☐ ☐ ☐ ☐ ☐

WATER VISIBILITY

CLEAR | 1 | 2 | 3 | 4 | 5 | MISTY

☐ ☐ ☐ ☐ ☐

TEAM / PADDLE PARTNER

☐	☐
☐	☐
☐	☐

BODY OF WATER

LAKE	OCEAN	CANAL
SEA	RIVER	OTHER

GEAR / EQUIPMENT

TRIP GOALS

OCEAN/BUOY/SURF/MARINE:

⊘ STOPS	🕐 TIME OF ARRIVAL	📄 OBSERVATIONS

ADDITIONAL NOTES

DATE: TIME:

STARTING POINT:

DESTINATION:

DISTANCE:

DURATION:

TEAM / PADDLE PARTNER

☐	☐
☐	☐
☐	☐

GEAR / EQUIPMENT

WEATHER CONDITIONS

TEMPERATURE _____ ☀ ⛅ ☁ 🌧 ❄

WIND _____ ☐ ☐ ☐ ☐ ☐

WATER VISIBILITY

CLEAR 1 2 3 4 5 MISTY

☐ ☐ ☐ ☐ ☐

BODY OF WATER

	LAKE		OCEAN		CANAL
	SEA		RIVER		OTHER

TRIP GOALS

OCEAN/BUOY/SURF/MARINE:

⊘ STOPS	⊘ TIME OF ARRIVAL	📄 OBSERVATIONS

ADDITIONAL NOTES

📅 DATE:	TIME:

📍 **STARTING POINT:**

📍 **DESTINATION:**

🕐 **DISTANCE:**

⏱ **DURATION:**

WEATHER CONDITIONS

🌡 TEMPERATURE _____	☀	⛅	☁	🌧	❄
🏳 WIND _____	☐	☐	☐	☐	☐

WATER VISIBILITY

CLEAR |‑‑‑1‑‑‑‑‑2‑‑‑‑‑3‑‑‑‑‑4‑‑‑‑‑5‑‑‑| MISTY

☐ ☐ ☐ ☐ ☐

👥 TEAM / PADDLE PARTNER

☐	☐
☐	☐
☐	☐

BODY OF WATER

LAKE	OCEAN	CANAL
SEA	RIVER	OTHER

GEAR / EQUIPMENT

TRIP GOALS

OCEAN/BUOY/SURF/MARINE:

📍 STOPS	🕐 TIME OF ARRIVAL	📄 OBSERVATIONS

ADDITIONAL NOTES

DATE:	TIME:

STARTING POINT:

DESTINATION:

DISTANCE:

DURATION:

TEAM / PADDLE PARTNER

	☐
	☐
	☐

GEAR / EQUIPMENT

WEATHER CONDITIONS

TEMPERATURE _____

WIND _____ ☐ ☐ ☐ ☐ ☐

WATER VISIBILITY

CLEAR 1   2   3   4   5 MISTY

☐ ☐ ☐ ☐ ☐

BODY OF WATER

	LAKE		OCEAN		CANAL
	SEA		RIVER		OTHER

TRIP GOALS

OCEAN/BUOY/SURF/MARINE:

⬦ STOPS	🕐 TIME OF ARRIVAL	📄 OBSERVATIONS

ADDITIONAL NOTES

📅 DATE:	TIME:

📍 STARTING POINT:

📍 DESTINATION:

🕐 DISTANCE:

⏱ DURATION:

WEATHER CONDITIONS

🌡 TEMPERATURE _____ ☀ ⛅ ☁ 🌦 ❄

🍃 WIND _____ ☐ ☐ ☐ ☐ ☐

WATER VISIBILITY

CLEAR	1	2	3	4	5	MISTY
	☐	☐	☐	☐	☐	

👥 TEAM / PADDLE PARTNER

☐	☐
☐	☐
☐	☐

BODY OF WATER

☐ LAKE	☐ OCEAN	☐ CANAL
☐ SEA	☐ RIVER	☐ OTHER

GEAR / EQUIPMENT

TRIP GOALS

OCEAN/BUOY/SURF/MARINE:

📍 STOPS	🕐 TIME OF ARRIVAL	📄 OBSERVATIONS

ADDITIONAL NOTES

DATE: **TIME:**

STARTING POINT:

DESTINATION:

DISTANCE:

DURATION:

TEAM / PADDLE PARTNER

☐	☐
☐	☐
☐	☐

GEAR / EQUIPMENT

WEATHER CONDITIONS

TEMPERATURE _____ ☀ ⛅ ☁ 🌧 ❄

WIND _____ ☐ ☐ ☐ ☐ ☐

WATER VISIBILITY

	1	2	3	4	5	
CLEAR						MISTY
	☐	☐	☐	☐	☐	

BODY OF WATER

☐ LAKE	☐ OCEAN	☐ CANAL
☐ SEA	☐ RIVER	☐ OTHER

TRIP GOALS

OCEAN/BUOY/SURF/MARINE:

⊘ STOPS	⊙ TIME OF ARRIVAL	🗎 OBSERVATIONS

ADDITIONAL NOTES

📅 DATE:	TIME:

📍 STARTING POINT:

☑ DESTINATION:

🕐 DISTANCE:

⏱ DURATION:

👥 TEAM / PADDLE PARTNER

☐	☐
☐	☐
☐	☐

GEAR / EQUIPMENT

WEATHER CONDITIONS

TEMPERATURE ____	☀	⛅	☁	🌧	❄
WIND ____	☐	☐	☐	☐	☐

WATER VISIBILITY

1	2	3	4	5
CLEAR				MISTY
☐	☐	☐	☐	☐

BODY OF WATER

LAKE	OCEAN	CANAL
SEA	RIVER	OTHER

TRIP GOALS

OCEAN/BUOY/SURF/MARINE:

📍 STOPS	🕐 TIME OF ARRIVAL	📄 OBSERVATIONS

ADDITIONAL NOTES

DATE: TIME:

STARTING POINT:

DESTINATION:

DISTANCE:

DURATION:

TEAM / PADDLE PARTNER

☐	☐
☐	☐
☐	☐

GEAR / EQUIPMENT

WEATHER CONDITIONS

TEMPERATURE _____ ☀ ⛅ ☁ 🌧 ❄

WIND _____ ☐ ☐ ☐ ☐ ☐

WATER VISIBILITY

	1	2	3	4	5	
CLEAR						MISTY
	☐	☐	☐	☐	☐	

BODY OF WATER

	LAKE		OCEAN		CANAL
	SEA		RIVER		OTHER

TRIP GOALS

OCEAN/BUOY/SURF/MARINE:

⦿ STOPS	⦿ TIME OF ARRIVAL	🗎 OBSERVATIONS

ADDITIONAL NOTES

📅 DATE:	TIME:

📍 **STARTING POINT:**

📍 **DESTINATION:**

🕐 **DISTANCE:**

⏱️ **DURATION:**

WEATHER CONDITIONS

🌡️ TEMPERATURE _____ ☀️ ⛅ ☁️ 🌧️ ❄️

🌬️ WIND _____ ☐ ☐ ☐ ☐ ☐

WATER VISIBILITY

	1	2	3	4	5	
CLEAR						MISTY
	☐	☐	☐	☐	☐	

👥 TEAM / PADDLE PARTNER

☐	☐
☐	☐
☐	☐

BODY OF WATER

☐ LAKE	☐ OCEAN	☐ CANAL
☐ SEA	☐ RIVER	☐ OTHER

GEAR / EQUIPMENT

TRIP GOALS

OCEAN/BUOY/SURF/MARINE:

📍 STOPS	🕐 TIME OF ARRIVAL	📄 OBSERVATIONS

ADDITIONAL NOTES

📅 DATE:	TIME:

📍 STARTING POINT:

🏁 DESTINATION:

🕐 DISTANCE:

⏱ DURATION:

👥 TEAM / PADDLE PARTNER

☐	☐
☐	☐
☐	☐

GEAR / EQUIPMENT

WEATHER CONDITIONS

🌡 TEMPERATURE _____	☀	⛅	☁	🌦	❄
💨 WIND _____	☐	☐	☐	☐	☐

WATER VISIBILITY

	1	2	3	4	5	
CLEAR						MISTY
	☐	☐	☐	☐	☐	

BODY OF WATER

☐ LAKE	☐ OCEAN	☐ CANAL
☐ SEA	☐ RIVER	☐ OTHER

TRIP GOALS

OCEAN/BUOY/SURF/MARINE:

📍 STOPS	🕐 TIME OF ARRIVAL	📄 OBSERVATIONS

ADDITIONAL NOTES

_____
_____
_____
_____
_____
_____

📅 DATE: _____ TIME: _____

📍 STARTING POINT: _____

📍 DESTINATION: _____

🕐 DISTANCE: _____

⏱ DURATION: _____

WEATHER CONDITIONS

🌡 TEMPERATURE _____ ☀ ⛅ ☁ 🌧 ❄

💨 WIND _____ ☐ ☐ ☐ ☐ ☐

WATER VISIBILITY

	1	2	3	4	5	
CLEAR						MISTY
	☐	☐	☐	☐	☐	

👥 TEAM / PADDLE PARTNER

☐	☐
☐	☐
☐	☐

BODY OF WATER

	LAKE		OCEAN		CANAL
	SEA		RIVER		OTHER

GEAR / EQUIPMENT

TRIP GOALS

OCEAN/BUOY/SURF/MARINE: _____

📍 STOPS	🕐 TIME OF ARRIVAL	📄 OBSERVATIONS

ADDITIONAL NOTES

_____

_____

_____

_____

_____

_____

	DATE:	TIME:

STARTING POINT:

DESTINATION:

DISTANCE:

DURATION:

TEAM / PADDLE PARTNER

⃝		⃝
⃝		⃝
⃝		⃝

GEAR / EQUIPMENT

WEATHER CONDITIONS

TEMPERATURE _____ ☀ ⛅ ☁ 🌧 ❄

WIND _____ ☐ ☐ ☐ ☐ ☐

WATER VISIBILITY

CLEAR |1____2____3____4____5| MISTY
☐ ☐ ☐ ☐ ☐

BODY OF WATER

LAKE	OCEAN	CANAL
SEA	RIVER	OTHER

TRIP GOALS

OCEAN/BUOY/SURF/MARINE:

⊘ STOPS	🕐 TIME OF ARRIVAL	OBSERVATIONS

ADDITIONAL NOTES

DATE: _____ TIME: _____

STARTING POINT: _____

DESTINATION: _____

DISTANCE: _____

DURATION: _____

WEATHER CONDITIONS

TEMPERATURE _____ ☼ ⛅ ☁ 🌧 ❄

WIND _____ ☐ ☐ ☐ ☐ ☐

WATER VISIBILITY

CLEAR | 1 | 2 | 3 | 4 | 5 | MIST

☐ ☐ ☐ ☐ ☐

TEAM / PADDLE PARTNER

☐	☐
☐	☐
☐	☐

BODY OF WATER

	LAKE		OCEAN		CANAL
	SEA		RIVER		OTHER

GEAR / EQUIPMENT

TRIP GOALS

OCEAN/BUOY/SURF/MARINE:

⊘ STOPS	⊘ TIME OF ARRIVAL	🗎 OBSERVATIONS

ADDITIONAL NOTES

	DATE:	TIME:

	STARTING POINT:

	DESTINATION:

	DISTANCE:

	DURATION:

TEAM / PADDLE PARTNER

☐	☐
☐	☐
☐	☐

GEAR / EQUIPMENT

WEATHER CONDITIONS

TEMPERATURE ___	☐	☐	☐	☐	☐
WIND ___	☐	☐	☐	☐	☐

WATER VISIBILITY

CLEAR | 1 | 2 | 3 | 4 | 5 | MISTY

| ☐ | ☐ | ☐ | ☐ | ☐ |

BODY OF WATER

LAKE	OCEAN	CANAL
SEA	RIVER	OTHER

TRIP GOALS

OCEAN/BUOY/SURF/MARINE:

⊙ STOPS	⊙ TIME OF ARRIVAL	🗎 OBSERVATIONS

ADDITIONAL NOTES

DATE:	**TIME:**

STARTING POINT:

DESTINATION:

DISTANCE:

DURATION:

TEAM / PADDLE PARTNER

☐	☐
☐	☐
☐	☐

GEAR / EQUIPMENT

WEATHER CONDITIONS

TEMPERATURE _____	☀	⛅	☁	🌧	❄
WIND _____	☐	☐	☐	☐	☐

WATER VISIBILITY

CLEAR	1	2	3	4	5	MISTY
	☐	☐	☐	☐	☐	

BODY OF WATER

LAKE	OCEAN	CANAL
SEA	RIVER	OTHER

TRIP GOALS

OCEAN/BUOY/SURF/MARINE:

⦿ STOPS	🕐 TIME OF ARRIVAL	📄 OBSERVATIONS

ADDITIONAL NOTES

DATE: **TIME:**

STARTING POINT:

DESTINATION:

DISTANCE:

DURATION:

TEAM / PADDLE PARTNER

	☐
	☐
	☐

GEAR / EQUIPMENT

WEATHER CONDITIONS

TEMPERATURE _____

WIND _____ ☐ ☐ ☐ ☐ ☐

WATER VISIBILITY

CLEAR | 1 | 2 | 3 | 4 | 5 | MISTY

☐   ☐   ☐   ☐   ☐

BODY OF WATER

LAKE	OCEAN	CANAL
SEA	RIVER	OTHER

TRIP GOALS

OCEAN/BUOY/SURF/MARINE:

⊘ STOPS	⊙ TIME OF ARRIVAL	🗎 OBSERVATIONS

ADDITIONAL NOTES

DATE:	TIME:

STARTING POINT:

DESTINATION:

DISTANCE:

DURATION:

WEATHER CONDITIONS

TEMPERATURE _____ ☼ ⛅ ☁ 🌧 ❄

WIND _____ ☐ ☐ ☐ ☐ ☐

WATER VISIBILITY

CLEAR 1 — 2 — 3 — 4 — 5 MIST

☐ ☐ ☐ ☐ ☐

TEAM / PADDLE PARTNER

☐	☐
☐	☐
☐	☐

BODY OF WATER

☐ LAKE	☐ OCEAN	☐ CANAL
☐ SEA	☐ RIVER	☐ OTHER

GEAR / EQUIPMENT

TRIP GOALS

OCEAN/BUOY/SURF/MARINE:

⊘ STOPS	⏱ TIME OF ARRIVAL	📄 OBSERVATIONS

ADDITIONAL NOTES

DATE: TIME:

📍 **STARTING POINT:**

DESTINATION:

DISTANCE:

DURATION:

👥 TEAM / PADDLE PARTNER

☐	☐
☐	☐
☐	☐

GEAR / EQUIPMENT

WEATHER CONDITIONS

TEMPERATURE _____ ☼ ⛅ ☁ 🌧 ❄

WIND _____ ☐ ☐ ☐ ☐ ☐

WATER VISIBILITY

1	2	3	4	5
CLEAR ──────────────────────── MISTY

☐ ☐ ☐ ☐ ☐

BODY OF WATER

☐ LAKE	☐ OCEAN	☐ CANAL
☐ SEA	☐ RIVER	☐ OTHER

TRIP GOALS

OCEAN/BUOY/SURF/MARINE:

📍 STOPS	🕐 TIME OF ARRIVAL	📄 OBSERVATIONS

ADDITIONAL NOTES

📅 DATE:	TIME:

STARTING POINT:

DESTINATION:

DISTANCE:

DURATION:

👥 TEAM / PADDLE PARTNER

☐	☐
☐	☐
☐	☐

GEAR / EQUIPMENT

WEATHER CONDITIONS

TEMPERATURE _____	☀	⛅	☁	🌧	❄
WIND _____	☐	☐	☐	☐	☐

WATER VISIBILITY

CLEAR | 1 | 2 | 3 | 4 | 5 | MISTY

| ☐ | ☐ | ☐ | ☐ | ☐ |

BODY OF WATER

LAKE	OCEAN	CANAL
SEA	RIVER	OTHER

TRIP GOALS

OCEAN/BUOY/SURF/MARINE:

⚲ STOPS	🕐 TIME OF ARRIVAL	📄 OBSERVATIONS

ADDITIONAL NOTES

	DATE:	TIME:

STARTING POINT:

DESTINATION:

DISTANCE:

DURATION:

TEAM / PADDLE PARTNER

	☐
	☐
	☐

GEAR / EQUIPMENT

WEATHER CONDITIONS

TEMPERATURE _____

WIND _____ ☐ ☐ ☐ ☐ ☐

WATER VISIBILITY

CLEAR 1 2 3 4 5 MISTY
☐ ☐ ☐ ☐ ☐

BODY OF WATER

	LAKE		OCEAN		CANAL
	SEA		RIVER		OTHER

TRIP GOALS

OCEAN/BUOY/SURF/MARINE:

◎ STOPS	◷ TIME OF ARRIVAL	🗎 OBSERVATIONS

ADDITIONAL NOTES

DATE: TIME:

STARTING POINT:

DESTINATION:

DISTANCE:

DURATION:

TEAM / PADDLE PARTNER

☐	☐
☐	☐
☐	☐

GEAR / EQUIPMENT

WEATHER CONDITIONS

TEMPERATURE _____ ☼ ⛅ ☁ 🌧 ❄

WIND _____ ☐ ☐ ☐ ☐ ☐

WATER VISIBILITY

CLEAR | 1   2   3   4   5 | MIST

☐   ☐   ☐   ☐   ☐

BODY OF WATER

LAKE	OCEAN	CANAL
SEA	RIVER	OTHER

TRIP GOALS

OCEAN/BUOY/SURF/MARINE:

⊘ STOPS	🕐 TIME OF ARRIVAL	🗎 OBSERVATIONS

ADDITIONAL NOTES

📅 DATE:	TIME:

📍 **STARTING POINT:**

📍 **DESTINATION:**

🕐 **DISTANCE:**

⏱ **DURATION:**

WEATHER CONDITIONS

🌡 TEMPERATURE _____ ☀ ⛅ ☁ 🌧 ❄

〰 WIND _____ ☐ ☐ ☐ ☐ ☐

WATER VISIBILITY

	1	2	3	4	5	
CLEAR						MISTY
	☐	☐	☐	☐	☐	

👥 TEAM / PADDLE PARTNER

☐	☐
☐	☐
☐	☐

BODY OF WATER

☐ LAKE	☐ OCEAN	☐ CANAL
☐ SEA	☐ RIVER	☐ OTHER

GEAR / EQUIPMENT

TRIP GOALS

OCEAN/BUOY/SURF/MARINE:

📍 STOPS	🕐 TIME OF ARRIVAL	📄 OBSERVATIONS

ADDITIONAL NOTES

	DATE:	TIME:

	STARTING POINT:

	DESTINATION:

	DISTANCE:

	DURATION:

WEATHER CONDITIONS

TEMPERATURE _____	☀	⛅	☁	🌧	❄
WIND _____	☐	☐	☐	☐	☐

WATER VISIBILITY

CLEAR | 1 | 2 | 3 | 4 | 5 | MISTY

☐ ☐ ☐ ☐ ☐

TEAM / PADDLE PARTNER

☐	☐
☐	☐
☐	☐

BODY OF WATER

	LAKE		OCEAN		CANAL
	SEA		RIVER		OTHER

GEAR / EQUIPMENT

TRIP GOALS

OCEAN/BUOY/SURF/MARINE:

⦿ STOPS	⦿ TIME OF ARRIVAL	📄 OBSERVATIONS

ADDITIONAL NOTES

DATE: **TIME:**

STARTING POINT:

DESTINATION:

DISTANCE:

DURATION:

TEAM / PADDLE PARTNER

	☐
	☐
	☐

GEAR / EQUIPMENT

WEATHER CONDITIONS

TEMPERATURE _____ ☀ ⛅ ☁ 🌧 ❄

WIND _____ ☐ ☐ ☐ ☐ ☐

WATER VISIBILITY

1	2	3	4	5
CLEAR   MISTY

☐   ☐   ☐   ☐   ☐

BODY OF WATER

	LAKE		OCEAN		CANAL
	SEA		RIVER		OTHER

TRIP GOALS

OCEAN/BUOY/SURF/MARINE:

⊘ STOPS	⏱ TIME OF ARRIVAL	📄 OBSERVATIONS

ADDITIONAL NOTES

📅 DATE:	TIME:

📍 STARTING POINT:

📍 DESTINATION:

🕐 DISTANCE:

⏱ DURATION:

WEATHER CONDITIONS

🌡 TEMPERATURE _____ ☀ 🌤 ☁ 🌧 ❄

🍃 WIND _____ ☐ ☐ ☐ ☐ ☐

WATER VISIBILITY

CLEAR	1	2	3	4	5	MIST
	☐	☐	☐	☐	☐	

👥 TEAM / PADDLE PARTNER

☐	☐
☐	☐
☐	☐

BODY OF WATER

LAKE	OCEAN	CANAL
SEA	RIVER	OTHER

GEAR / EQUIPMENT

TRIP GOALS

OCEAN/BUOY/SURF/MARINE:

📍 STOPS	🕐 TIME OF ARRIVAL	📄 OBSERVATIONS

ADDITIONAL NOTES

DATE:	TIME:

STARTING POINT:

DESTINATION:

DISTANCE:

DURATION:

TEAM / PADDLE PARTNER

☐	☐
☐	☐
☐	☐

GEAR / EQUIPMENT

WEATHER CONDITIONS

TEMPERATURE _____ ☼ ⛅ ☁ 🌧 ❄

WIND _____ ☐ ☐ ☐ ☐ ☐

WATER VISIBILITY

1	2	3	4	5
CLEAR ═══════════════════ MISTY

☐ ☐ ☐ ☐ ☐

BODY OF WATER

☐ LAKE	☐ OCEAN	☐ CANAL
☐ SEA	☐ RIVER	☐ OTHER

TRIP GOALS

OCEAN/BUOY/SURF/MARINE:

⊙ STOPS	⊙ TIME OF ARRIVAL	▤ OBSERVATIONS

ADDITIONAL NOTES

DATE: TIME:

STARTING POINT:

DESTINATION:

DISTANCE:

DURATION:

WEATHER CONDITIONS

TEMPERATURE _____

WIND _____

☐ ☐ ☐ ☐ ☐

WATER VISIBILITY

| 1 | 2 | 3 | 4 | 5 |
CLEAR   MISTY

☐ ☐ ☐ ☐ ☐

TEAM / PADDLE PARTNER

☐	☐
☐	☐
☐	☐

BODY OF WATER

LAKE	OCEAN	CANAL
SEA	RIVER	OTHER

GEAR / EQUIPMENT

TRIP GOALS

OCEAN/BUOY/SURF/MARINE:

📍 STOPS	🕐 TIME OF ARRIVAL	📄 OBSERVATIONS

ADDITIONAL NOTES

DATE:	TIME:

STARTING POINT:

DESTINATION:

DISTANCE:

DURATION:

TEAM / PADDLE PARTNER

	☐
	☐
	☐

GEAR / EQUIPMENT

WEATHER CONDITIONS

TEMPERATURE ____ ☀ ⛅ ☁ 🌧 ❄

WIND ____ ☐ ☐ ☐ ☐ ☐

WATER VISIBILITY

	1	2	3	4	5	
CLEAR						MISTY
	☐	☐	☐	☐	☐	

BODY OF WATER

	LAKE		OCEAN		CANAL
	SEA		RIVER		OTHER

TRIP GOALS

OCEAN/BUOY/SURF/MARINE:

⊘ STOPS	⊙ TIME OF ARRIVAL	📄 OBSERVATIONS

ADDITIONAL NOTES

📅 DATE:	TIME:

📍 STARTING POINT:

📍 DESTINATION:

🕐 DISTANCE:

⏱ DURATION:

WEATHER CONDITIONS

🌡 TEMPERATURE _____ ☀ ⛅ ☁ 🌧 ❄

🌬 WIND _____ ☐ ☐ ☐ ☐ ☐

WATER VISIBILITY

	1	2	3	4	5	
CLEAR						MIST
	☐	☐	☐	☐	☐	

👥 TEAM / PADDLE PARTNER

☐	☐
☐	☐
☐	☐

BODY OF WATER

☐ LAKE	☐ OCEAN	☐ CANAL
☐ SEA	☐ RIVER	☐ OTHER

GEAR / EQUIPMENT

TRIP GOALS

OCEAN/BUOY/SURF/MARINE:

📍 STOPS	🕐 TIME OF ARRIVAL	📄 OBSERVATIONS

ADDITIONAL NOTES

NOTES 📄

NOTES 📄

NOTES 📄

NOTES

NOTES 📄

NOTES

NOTES

NOTES

NOTES 📄

NOTES 📄

NOTES

NOTES

NOTES

NOTES 📄

Printed in Great Britain
by Amazon

37002119R00077